LEVEL
3
Fact Reader

Squeak!

100 FUN Facts About Hamsters, Mice, Guinea Pigs, and More

Rose Davidson

NATIONAL GEOGRAPHIC

Washington, D.C.

For Brady —R.D.

Designed by Nicole Lazarus, Design Superette

Library of Congress Cataloging-in-Publication Data
Names: Davidson, Rose, 1989- author. | National
   Geographic Society (U.S.)
Title: National Geographic readers : squeak! / by Rose
   Davidson.
Other titles: Squeak!
Description: Washington, DC : National Geographic
   Kids, [2019] | Series: National Geographic readers |
   Audience: Age 6-9. | Audience: K to Grade 3.
Identifiers: LCCN 2018057781 (print) | LCCN 2018058868
   (ebook) | ISBN 9781426334900 (e-book) | ISBN
   9781426334887 (paperback) | ISBN 9781426334894
   (hardcover)
Subjects: LCSH: Rodents--Juvenile literature.
Classification: LCC QL737.R6 (ebook) | LCC QL737.R6
   D27 2019 (print) | DDC 599.35--dc23
LC record available at https://lccn.loc.gov/2018057781

The author and publisher gratefully acknowledge the expert content review of this book by Matt Mulligan, small mammal expert, wildlife research coordinator, Davee Center for Epidemiology and Endocrinology, Urban Wildlife Institute, Lincoln Park Zoo, and the literacy review of this book by Mariam Jean Dreher, professor of reading education, University of Maryland, College Park.

Photo Credits
GI=Getty Images; MP=Minden Pictures; NGIC= National Geographic Image Collection; SS=Shutterstock

Cover, Photostock-Israel/GI; header throughout (assorted rodents), Thumbelina/SS; (mice), nemlaza/SS; (squirrels), Potapov Alexander/SS; 1, Warren Metcalf/SS; 3, David Liittschwager/NGIC; 4 (UP), Joel Sartore/NGIC; 4 (CTR), Tony Campbell/SS; 4 (LO LE), Robert Harding Picture Library/NGIC; 4-5 (LO), Henk Bentlage/SS; 5 (UP LE), rvlsoft/SS; 5 (UP RT), S & D & K Maslowski/FLPA/SS; 5 (CTR RT), Viachaslau Kraskouski/SS; 5 (LO RT), shot by supervliegzus/GI; 6, Poly Liss/SS; 7, Vishnevskiy Vasily/SS; 8, Misja Smits/MP; 9 (UP), Neil Bromhall/SS; 9 (CTR), stanley45/GI; 9 (LO), Heidi and Hans-Juergen Koch/MP; 10, Alouise Lynch; 11, Joe McDonald/Steve Bloom Images/Alamy Stock Photo; 12, Tom Reichner/SS; 13 (UP), Richard Seeley/SS; 13 (CTR), Robert Eastman/SS; 13 (LO), Eric Isselée/SS; 14, Mike Walker/SS; 15 (UP), Lehtikuva/SS; 15 (LO), Will & Deni Mcintyre/GI; 16, Dave Bevan/Alamy Stock Photo; 17 (UP), Clark Little/SWNS; 17 (LO), Aneta Jungerova/SS; 18, Xavier ROSSI/Gamma-Rapho via GI; 19 (UP), Carl De Souza/AFP/GI; 19 (CTR), Alexander Joe/AFP/GI; 19 (LO LE), Duncan Noakes/Dreamstime; 19 (LO RT), Jagodka/SS; 20 (LE), Dr. Charline Couchoux; 20 (RT), Maxime Aubert/NGIC; 21, David Liittschwager/NGIC; 22-23, Michael Forsberg/NGIC; 24, Caglar Gungor/Dreamstime; 25, Ens Schlueter/AFP/GI; 26-27, Charlie Hamilton James/NGIC; 27 (UP), Suzi Eszterhas/MP; 27 (LO), Charlie Hamilton James/NGIC; 28, R Hermes/MP; 28-29, Farinosa/GI; 30, Nicola Destefano/GI; 31, hakoar/GI; 32, Brian E Kushner/SS; 33, Philippe Henry/GI; 34, Erlend Haarberg/Nature Picture Library; 35 (UP), Wibke Woyke/Alamy Stock Photo; 35 (LO), Mint Images/REX/SS; 36, Stefan Huwiler/GI; 37 (UP), Africa Studio/SS; 37 (LO), Photostock-Israel/GI; 38, Paul Starosta/GI; 39 (UP), Heidi and Hans-Juergen Koch/MP; 39 (LO), Tierfotoagentur/S. Schwerdtfeger/Alamy Stock Photo; 40, Nataly Go/GI; 41 (UP), Valerieka/SS; 41 (LO), Becky Matthews/Alamy Stock Photo; 42-43, Stock image/SS; 44 (UP LE), Ultrashock/SS; 44 (UP RT), Jay Dickman/NGIC; 44 (LO LE), Voren1/GI; 44 (LO RT), Eric Isselée/SS; 45 (UP), Valeriy Maleev/Nature Picture Library; 45 (CTR LE), Philippe Henry/MP; 45 (CTR RT), Tatiane Noviski Fornel/GI; 45 (LO), Inkwelldodo/Dreamstime

National Geographic supports K–12 educators with ELA Common Core Resources. Visit natgeoed.org/commoncore for more information.

Printed in the United States of America
19/WOR/1

Table of Contents

1. The naked mole rat can live more than 30 years, longer than any other rodent species.

2. There are more than 2,200 rodent species on Earth today, and scientists are still discovering new species.

3. Sometimes mice squeak at a frequency so high that humans can't hear it.

4. The Inca kept guinea pigs as pets more than 3,000 years ago in Peru.

5. Beavers make a goo that smells like vanilla.

6. The town of Olney, Illinois, U.S.A., is known as "the home of the white squirrels."

7. Some newborn mice, called pinkies, are so tiny they could fit in a bottle cap.

8. The house mouse usually lives near humans and can be found on every continent except Antarctica.

9. Prairie dogs live in communities called dog towns, each with hundreds of members.

10. Porcupines are born with soft quills, which harden after a few days.

25 COOL FACTS ABOUT RODENTS

11 Although it's not common, rats can swim up into toilets.

12 A mouse can eat 15 to 20 times a day.

13 Flying squirrels have parachute-like skin flaps that help them glide through the air from tree to tree.

14 Guinea pigs "popcorn," or rapidly run and jump around, when they're happy and healthy.

15 Vangunu giant rats—recently discovered in the Solomon Islands—eat coconuts.

16 Gerbils "thump" their back legs to warn other gerbils of possible danger.

17 The three-foot-long Indian giant squirrel has fur in shades of black, brown, orange, maroon, and purple.

18 The Patagonian mara can run at speeds of 28 miles an hour.

19 There are 18 species of hamsters, but only five are kept as pets.

20 Guinea pigs can walk immediately after they're born.

21 The agouti (ah-GOO-tee) is the only animal that can crack open a Brazil nut with its teeth.

22 The African spiny mouse can shed its tail skin to escape a predator.

23 Chinchillas roll around in dust from volcanoes to stay clean.

24 Capybaras are social animals and get along with many other species, including birds, turtles, and monkeys.

25 A female house mouse can give birth to 10 litters a year, usually with five to seven young in each litter.

CHAPTER 1

RODENTS RULE

Rodents are the LARGEST GROUP OF MAMMALS on Earth.

By digging tunnels, PRAIRIE DOGS MIX UP SOIL, which helps plants grow.

Rodents are real-life superheroes of the animal kingdom. Prairie dogs help keep soil healthy. Beavers build dams that form new habitats. Rats even detect disease, which helps save human lives.

About 40 percent of all mammals are rodents. Mammals are warm-blooded animals with hair. They give birth to live young and nurse their babies with milk.

Rats can swim for THREE DAYS STRAIGHT.

Rodents' teeth NEVER STOP GROWING.

If there's one thing that sets rodents apart from other kinds of mammals, it's their chompers. Rodents cut things with special front teeth called incisors (in-SIGH-zers). The incisors grow for their entire lives.

A naked mole rat can move its incisors one at a time, and work them together LIKE A PAIR OF CHOPSTICKS.

These teeth help them survive. Rodents keep their incisors sharp and short by gnawing (NAW-ing) on wood and other tough plant matter.

beaver

Most rodents HAVE 16 TEETH—eight on top and eight on bottom. All but four are so far back, they're hard to see.

The name "RODENT" COMES FROM THE LATIN WORD for "gnaw."

9

African pygmy mouse

African pygmy mice have to EAT LOTS OF INSECTS to get enough protein.

Rodents come in many sizes. African pygmy mice weigh about the same as a wooden pencil. They live in dry areas, where they stack pebbles outside their burrows. The pebbles collect dew overnight. In the morning when the mice wake up, they lick the dew to get water.

capybaras

Capybaras, however, are the giants of the rodent world. These South American rodents can grow to be the size of some large dogs—more than 150 pounds! They live in herds of up to 20 individuals.

Capybara herds are LED BY A DOMINANT MALE.

Fooled You!

Some animals are commonly confused with rodents—and it's easy to see why. Here's the truth about these rodent look-alikes.

RABBITS AND HARES: An extra pair of incisor teeth sets these animals apart from true rodents. This animal group is known as lagomorphs (LAH-guh-morfs).

PIKAS: The cute and furry pika (PIE-kah) is another kind of lagomorph. It's the smallest of its kind.

HEDGEHOGS: Even though they have quills like porcupines—which are rodents—hedgehogs are more closely related to shrews.

While a hedgehog isn't a rodent, the spiny mouse is! It has STIFF HAIRS ON ITS BACK FOR DEFENSE.

Rodents and lagomorphs BOTH LIKE EATING PLANTS—but some rodents also eat other animals.

CHAPTER 2

AMAZING ABILITIES

Rodents are some of the animal world's
MOST SKILLED PROBLEM-SOLVERS.

Have you ever watched a squirrel snag
the seeds from inside a bird feeder? Then
you've seen a rodent's problem-solving
skills in action.

The
WIRING OF
A MOUSE'S BRAIN
CHANGES when it
learns a new
skill.

Rats can FIND
THEIR WAY OUT
OF MAZES.

Some rodents try out new solutions to
a problem until they find one that works.
They can remember how to solve a
specific problem—like how to push or
pull a lever to open a door—for years
after they first solved it.

Rats get a bad rap—but there are plenty of good things you may not know about them! Rats are supersmart. Scientists consider rats to be some of the most intelligent rodents. Some studies show they can learn to count. They can even tell when another rat is hurt, just by looking at its face.

Pet rats named Fin and Tofu LEARNED HOW TO RIDE A SURFBOARD IN HAWAII, U.S.A.

A group of rats is CALLED A MISCHIEF.

Rats to the Rescue

Rats use their superb sniffers to SAVE HUMAN LIVES.

Rats aren't just good at looking out for each other. Their talents can help people, too!

Rat noses are top-notch. With proper training, they can sniff out diseases like tuberculosis (tuh-BUR-kyuh-LOH-sis) and find things hidden deep underground.

Rats can tell if a lab sample has tuberculosis faster than humans can.

African giant pouched rats use their sense of smell to detect land mines buried in the dirt. Because they don't weigh much, the rats can walk over the mines without setting them off.

Rats have the SECOND HIGHEST NUMBER OF GENES that help them identify a smell. African elephants have the highest.

Critter Chatter

Chipmunks have worn mini spy gear
TO RECORD THEIR COMMUNICATIONS.

In addition to spy collars, another kind of microphone helps scientist Charline Couchoux collect recordings.

Chipmunks are super chatty—but for a long time, no humans knew what they were saying. Then one day, a scientist decided it was time to decode the chipmunk chatter.

One chipmunk can GATHER 165 ACORNS IN A SINGLE DAY.

She strapped tiny microphones to a handful of chipmunks in a Canadian forest. Then she waited and recorded what she heard.

She discovered that different sounds meant different things:

CHUCK: An alarm sound made when there's a predator in the sky

CHIP-TRILL: A high-pitched sound made when running to defend territory

TRILL: A sound made when surprised by a predator

CHIP: An alarm sound made when there's a predator on land

21

A prairie dog's call can tell others the SIZE, SHAPE, COLOR, AND SPEED OF A PREDATOR.

Like chipmunks, prairie dogs use many different calls. Some scientists say prairie dogs even have their own language.

Prairie dogs live in open areas where they're easy to spot. To warn each other of predators, they use a system of alerts.

When one prairie dog jumps and yips, OTHERS IN THE COLONY JOIN IN.

Prairie dogs GOT THEIR NAME FROM THE BARKING SOUND they make.

One type of call can tell other prairie dogs whether the predator is a coyote or a human. Prairie dogs can even make different calls depending on a human's shirt color. The calls sound different depending on the situation.

Prairie dogs LIVE TOGETHER BY THE HUNDREDS in their grassland habitat.

CHAPTER 3

WILD RODENTS

Researchers think the jerboa's LONG EARS RELEASE HEAT to keep it cool in its desert home.

The jerboa's hopping is hard to miss. But there's a lot we still don't know about these mysterious animals. For example, why do these desert rodents hop?

Scientists think hopping might help jerboas escape predators. By zigging and zagging, the jerboa makes it harder for predators in the sky to find and catch it on the ground. The jerboa hops away to safety in its desert home. Other rodents have different behaviors depending on where they live.

Jerboas DON'T DRINK WATER. They get it from the plants and insects they eat.

25

Beavers can stay UNDERWATER FOR 15 MINUTES before coming up for air.

Beavers spend some of their time on land, and the rest in the water. The dams they build raise water levels in streams to make ponds. These ponds help other animals survive in wetland areas.

To build a dam, beavers' bodies need to work well underwater. Beavers' eyelids are see-through and act like goggles. They help the animals see in the water. Their noses and ears close to keep water out. And beavers' lips close behind their teeth so they can carry things without letting in water.

Beavers STORE FAT IN THEIR TAILS. Their bodies use the fat in the winter to survive and stay warm.

WEBBED BACK FEET and a big, flat tail help beavers swim.

For some rodents, their strength is in their tail. Brazilian porcupines have grasping, or prehensile (pree-HEN-suhl), tails. This means they can use their tail to hang on to things. That's good, because these porcupines rarely come down to the ground. They eat and sleep in the trees.

Brazilian porcupines communicate with MOANS, WHINES, GRUNTS, SHRIEKS, and BARKS.

Brazilian porcupine

Even in the trees, these porcupines have to beware of predators. Short, thick quills cover the porcupines' bodies. The quills usually lie flat. But when a porcupine is disturbed, it shakes its quills to warn a predator: Back off!

A North American porcupine can have MORE THAN 30,000 QUILLS ON ITS BODY.

Home Sweet Burrow

Alpine marmot families CAN LIVE IN THE SAME BURROW FOR GENERATIONS.

You can see them in the
trees and by the water—but
where else do rodents live? In
their cold mountain habitat, alpine
marmots make their homes in burrows in
the ground. Inside, they huddle together
to stay warm. When winter
comes, the marmots
hibernate here.

Marmots also raise
their babies here.
When the young
marmots grow up,
the burrow will
become home for
their families, too.
Usually 15 to 20
marmots live in a
single burrow.

Marmots
TAKE CARE OF
EACH OTHER by
grooming.

Groundhogs have SHARP CLAWS for digging burrows.

A groundhog's burrow can have up to TWO DOZEN ENTRANCES.

When groundhogs hibernate, their hearts may ONLY BEAT FIVE TIMES A MINUTE.

Not all hibernating rodents live in big groups. Groundhogs usually live alone in their burrows. But like other animals that hibernate, their bodies change to save energy. Their heart slows down and their body temperature drops.

In summer and fall, groundhogs stuff themselves with fruits, grasses, and bark. They can eat a whole pound of food in just one sitting! In the winter, when it's time to hibernate, they survive off the fat they've stored from their feasts.

Groundhogs and marmots aren't the only rodents that live in burrows. Here are a few more underground rodents.

LEMMINGS: These mostly Arctic rodents don't hibernate, but they do use burrows. Lemmings give birth in underground burrows year-round.

Blesmols have BARREL-SHAPED BODIES that help them move through tunnels.

BLESMOLS (BLESS-MOLES): Because they feed on plant roots, bulbs, and tubers belowground, these African rodents can destroy crops. They are often considered pests.

PACAS: Piglike rodents called pacas build their burrows near water in Central and South America.

While pacas might be a bit CLUMSY ON LAND, they're GREAT SWIMMERS.

CHAPTER 4

FURRY FRIENDS

European hamster

WILD HAMSTERS still live in Europe and Asia.

Hamsters are some of the most popular rodent pets. But before they were pets, they were wild animals! In the 1930s, a researcher from Jerusalem brought home a few hamsters from an expedition. The hamsters quickly reproduced—and the rest is history.

Today, there are still wild hamsters around the world. Pet hamsters are bred to be pets. It's important for wild hamsters, and other wild rodents, to stay in the wild.

A golden hamster litter can have MORE THAN 20 PUPS.

These animals can really turn up the cute. Their cheeks are like inflated balloons when they're filled with foods like fruits, veggies, and leafy greens. They can pack up to a fifth of their body weight into their mouths!

Mother hamsters sometimes HIDE THEIR BABIES IN THEIR CHEEKS to protect them from harm.

What hamsters lack in table manners, they make up for in grooming. Hamsters comb and lick their hair to stay clean.

Rodent Roommates

You might be tempted to share your room with your pet pal. But before you do, know this: While you're trying to sleep, your furry friend might be wide awake. That's because lots of rodents are nocturnal, or active at night. Others are crepuscular (kreh-PUH-skyuh-ler), or active at dawn and dusk. In the wild, this helps them avoid daytime predators—but at home, it could mean noisy nights.

Short periods of DIRECT SUNLIGHT are good for rodents' overall health.

Keeping your rodent friend happy and healthy means giving it a chance to be a little wild. Toys like running wheels keep a rodent active. Boxes and tubes give it places to hide. Treats to gnaw on keep your rodent's teeth short and sharp.

Wild rodents are clever and helpful. They build dams and help plants grow. Pet rodents can be helpful, too. Having a pet rodent can be fun and rewarding. No matter where they live, rodents have the power to make our lives better. Now that's something to squeak about!

Some RODENTS HELP NEW TREES GROW by spreading seeds as they move.

Because THEY HAVE POOR EYESIGHT, rodents rely more on senses like smell and touch to get around.

1. In case a porcupine accidentally pokes itself, its quills are covered in antibiotics to prevent infection.

2. Held every February 2 in the United States, Groundhog Day features a rodent named Punxsutawney Phil.

3. Brown rats can jump five times their body length—around four feet!

4. Rats can squeeze through tiny openings just over a half-inch wide.

5. Hamsters will fight each other for territory.

6. The Bosavi woolly rat—first discovered in the crater of an extinct volcano—is as big as a house cat.

7. A beaver's home is called a lodge. It's built of branches and mud and can be 40 feet wide.

8. Used to store food, a pocket gopher's cheek pouches extend all the way to its shoulders.

9. Scientists have studied capybaras' DNA for its cancer-fighting properties.

10. Nutria, rodents that look like beavers, were brought to the United States in the late 1800s for their fur.

11. To survive, meadow voles have to eat their weight in food every day.

12. Gerbils can be brown, black, gray, yellow, or white.

25 MORE FACTS ABOUT RODENTS

13

Rats can chew through cinder blocks, aluminum, and lead.

14

A long-eared jerboa's ears are two-thirds the length of its body.

15

Groundhogs, also called woodchucks, are the largest members of the squirrel family.

16

Now extinct, a prehistoric giant beaver was about the size of a black bear.

17

Muskrats can swim backward and forward.

18

Some wild gerbils live in deserts on the continents of Africa and Asia.

19

The fear of mice and rats is called musophobia (MUH-soh-FOH-bee-uh).

20

Prairie dogs touch noses and lock teeth to "kiss," which can tell them if they're part of the same group.

21

Tuco-tucos, native to South America, have orange enamel that protects their teeth.

22

The pacarana—a rare, slow-moving rodent species—lives only in the rainforests of northwestern South America.

23

Kangaroo rats have pouches on the sides of their mouth for carrying seeds.

24

Male degus (DAY-goos) build piles of sticks, rocks, and dung outside their burrows to show their status in a group.

25

"Cavy" is another name for a guinea pig.

RODENT FACTS ROUNDUP

EEEK!
You've gnawed through lots of rodent facts. Did you catch all 100?

1. The naked mole rat can live more than 30 years, longer than any other rodent species. 2. There are more than 2,200 rodent species on Earth today, and scientists are still discovering new species. 3. Sometimes mice squeak at a frequency so high that humans can't hear it. 4. The Inca kept guinea pigs as pets more than 3,000 years ago in Peru. 5. Beavers make a goo that smells like vanilla. 6. The town of Olney, Illinois, U.S.A., is known as "the home of the white squirrels." 7. Some newborn mice, called pinkies, are so tiny they could fit in a bottle cap. 8. The house mouse usually lives near humans and can be found on every continent except Antarctica. 9. Prairie dogs live in communities called dog towns, each with hundreds of members. 10. Porcupines are born with soft quills, which harden after a few days. 11. Although it's not common, rats can swim up into toilets. 12. A mouse can eat 15 to 20 times a day. 13. Flying squirrels have parachute-like skin flaps that help them glide through the air from tree to tree. 14. Guinea pigs "popcorn," or rapidly run and jump around, when they're happy and healthy. 15. Vangunu giant rats—recently discovered in the Solomon Islands—eat coconuts. 16. Gerbils "thump" their back legs to warn other gerbils of possible danger. 17. The three-foot-long Indian giant squirrel has fur in shades of black, brown, orange, maroon, and purple. 18. The Patagonian mara can run at speeds of 28 miles an hour. 19. There are 18 species of hamsters, but only five are kept as pets. 20. Guinea pigs can walk immediately after they're born. 21. The agouti (ah-GOO-tee) is the only animal that can crack open a Brazil nut with its teeth. 22. The African spiny mouse can shed its tail skin to escape a predator. 23. Chinchillas roll around in dust from volcanoes to stay clean. 24. Capybaras are social animals and get along with many other species—including birds, turtles, and monkeys. 25. A female house mouse can give birth to 10 litters a year, usually with five to seven young in each litter. 26. Rodents are the largest group of mammals on Earth. 27. By digging tunnels, prairie dogs mix up soil, which helps plants grow. 28. Rats can swim for three days straight. 29. Rodents' teeth never stop growing. 30. A naked mole rat can move its incisors one at a time, and work them together like a pair of chopsticks. 31. Most rodents have 16 teeth—eight on top, and eight on bottom. All but four are so far back, they're hard to see. 32. The name "rodent" comes from the Latin word for "gnaw." 33. African pygmy mice have to eat lots of insects to get enough protein. 34. Capybara herds are led by a dominant male. 35. Rodents and lagomorphs both like eating plants—but some rodents also eat other animals. 36. While a hedgehog isn't a rodent, the spiny mouse is! It has stiff hairs on its back for defense. 37. Rodents are some of the animal world's most skilled problem solvers. 38. The wiring of a mouse's brain changes when it learns a new skill. 39. Rats can find their way out of mazes. 40. Pet rats named Fin and Tofu learned how to ride a surfboard in Hawaii, U.S.A. 41. A group of rats is called a mischief. 42. Rats use their superb sniffers to save

human lives. 43. Rats have the second highest number of genes that help them identify a smell. African elephants have the highest. 44. Chipmunks have worn mini spy gear to record their communications. 45. One chipmunk can gather 165 acorns in a single day. 46. Chipmunks live in many habitats, including plains, mountains, forests, and deserts. 47. A prairie dog's call can tell others the size, shape, color, and speed of a predator. 48. When one prairie dog jumps and yips, others in the colony join in. 49. Prairie dogs got their name from the barking sound they make. 50. Prairie dogs live together by the hundreds in their grassland habitat. 51. Researchers think the jerboa's long ears release heat to keep it cool in its desert home. 52. Jerboas (jer-BOH-uhs) zigzag through the desert on kangaroo-like legs. 53. Jerboas don't drink water. They get it from the plants and insects they eat. 54. Beavers can stay underwater for 15 minutes before coming up for air. 55. Beavers store fat in their tails. Their bodies use the fat in the winter to survive and stay warm. 56. Webbed back feet and a big, flat tail help beavers swim. 57. Brazilian porcupines hang by their tails from tree branches. 58. Brazilian porcupines communicate with moans, whines, grunts, shrieks, and barks. 59. A North American porcupine can have more than 30,000 quills on its body. 60. Alpine marmot families can live in the same burrow for generations. 61. Like lots of rodents, alpine marmots can eat plants that would be poisonous to other mammals. 62. Marmots take care of each other by grooming. 63. Groundhogs have sharp claws for digging burrows. 64. A groundhog's burrow can have up to two dozen entrances. 65. When groundhogs hibernate, their hearts may only beat five times a minute. 66. Blesmols have barrel-shaped bodies that help them move through tunnels. 67. While pacas might be a bit clumsy on land, they're great swimmers. 68. Wild hamsters still live in Europe and Asia. 69. The most popular kind of pet hamsters, called golden hamsters or teddy bear hamsters, originally came from the country of Syria. 70. A golden hamster litter can have more than 20 pups. 71. Hamsters can stuff enough food in their cheeks to make their faces double in size. 72. Mother hamsters sometimes hide their babies in their cheeks to protect them from harm. 73. Short periods of direct sunlight are good for rodents' overall health. 74. Some rodents help new trees grow by spreading seeds as they move. 75. Because they have poor eyesight, rodents rely more on senses like smell and touch to get around. 76. In case a porcupine accidentally pokes itself, its quills are covered in antibiotics to prevent infection. 77. Held every February 2 in the United States, Groundhog Day features a rodent named Punxsutawney Phil. 78. Brown rats can jump five times their body length—around four feet! 79. Rats can squeeze through tiny openings just over a half-inch wide. 80. Hamsters will fight each other for territory. 81. The Bosavi woolly rat—first discovered in the crater of an extinct volcano—is as big as a house cat. 82. A beaver's home is called a lodge. It's built of branches and mud and can be 40 feet wide. 83. Used to store food, a pocket gopher's cheek pouches extend all the way to its shoulders. 84. Scientists have studied capybaras' DNA for its cancer-fighting properties. 85. Nutria, rodents that look like beavers, were brought to the United States in the late 1800s for their fur. 86. To survive, meadow voles have to eat their weight in food every day. 87. Gerbils can be brown, black, gray, yellow, or white. 88. Rats can chew through cinder blocks, aluminum, and lead. 89. A long-eared jerboa's ears are two-thirds the length of its body. 90. Groundhogs, also called woodchucks, are the largest members of the squirrel family. 91. Now extinct, a prehistoric giant beaver was about the size of a black bear. 92. Muskrats can swim backward and forward. 93. Some wild gerbils live in deserts on the continents of Africa and Asia. 94. The fear of mice and rats is called musophobia (MUH-soh-FOH-bee-uh). 95. Prairie dogs touch noses and lock teeth to "kiss," which can tell them if they're part of the same group. 96. Tuco-tucos, native to South America, have orange enamel that protects their teeth. 97. The pacarana—a rare, slow-moving rodent species—lives only in the rainforests of northwestern South America. 98. Kangaroo rats have pouches on the sides of their mouth for carrying seeds. 99. Male degus (DAY-goos) build piles of sticks, rocks, and dung outside their burrows to show their status in a group. 100. "Cavy" is another name for guinea pig.

INDEX

Boldface indicates illustrations.